SOCCER'S BIGGEST RIVALRIES

by Dani Borden

CAPSTONE PRESS

a capstone imprint

Published by Capstone Press, an imprint of Capstone
1710 Roe Crest Drive, North Mankato, Minnesota 56003
capstonepub.com

SPORTS ILLUSTRATED KIDS is a trademark of ABG-SI LLC. Used with permission.

Library of Congress Cataloging-in-Publication Data
Names: Borden, Dani, author.
Title: Soccer's biggest rivalries / by Dani Borden.
Description: North Mankato, Minnesota : Capstone Press, [2024] | Series: Sports
Illustrated Kids | Includes bibliographical references and index. | Audience: Ages 8
to 11 | Audience: Grades 4-6 | Summary: "The most popular sport in the world is
guaranteed to have its fair share of rivalries. Does winning a World Cup make a
team the best? Or does Olympic gold deserve the glory? Discover some of soccer's
biggest rivalries past and present and decide for yourself who's the best."—
Provided by publisher.
Identifiers: LCCN 2022050164 (print) | LCCN 2022050165 (ebook) | ISBN
9781669049173 (hardcover) | ISBN 9781669049128 (paperback) | ISBN
9781669049135 (pdf) | ISBN 9781669049159 (kindle edition) | ISBN
9781669049166 (epub)
Subjects: LCSH: Soccer—History—Juvenile literature. | Soccer teams—History—
Juvenile literature. | Sports rivalries—Juvenile literature.
Classification: LCC GV943.25 .B66 2024 (print) | LCC GV943.25 (ebook) | DDC
796.334/64—dc23
LC record available at https://lccn.loc.gov/2022050164
LC ebook record available at https://lccn.loc.gov/2022050165

Editorial Credits
Editor: Alison Deering; Designer: Elyse White; Media Researcher:
Rebekah Hubstenberger; Production Specialist: Whitney Schaefer

Image Credits
Alamy: Joe Scarnici/ZUMAPRESS.com, 22; Associated Press: CHRISTOPHE SAIDI/
SIPA, 13, Tom Gannam, 6; Getty Images: Ben Radford/Allsport, 28, Bob Kupbens/
Icon Sportswire, 23, Bob Thomas, 21, 29, David Ramos, 18, Denis Doyle, 4,
DOUGLAS MAGNO/AFP, 16, iStock/Invision Frame Studio, design element (soccer
ball icon), Michael Regan, 5, 20, PATRICK KOVARIK/AFP, 24, Robin Alam/Icon
Sportswire, 14, Ryan Pierse, 11, Simon Bruty/Anychance, 15, TOMMY CHENG/AFP,
12, ullstein bild, 26, Victor Carretero, 27; Newscom: Andy Mead/Icon SMI 918m,
10, imageBROKER/uwe kraft, cover (middle right); Shutterstock: Jansx Customs,
design element (lines), QueenArsyi, design element (soccer ball icon), vectortatu,
design element (vs.); Sports Illustrated: Simon Bruty, cover (middle left); University
of Wisconsin Milwaukee: Milwaukee Athletic Communications, 8, 9

All internet sites appearing in back matter were available and accurate
when this book was sent to press.

TABLE OF CONTENTS

Words in **bold** are in the glossary.

Kickoff!

Soccer is the number-one sport in the world. That attention can create intense rivalries between fans, players, and teams.

What drives a rivalry? It can be a team's location, neighbor playing against neighbor, or fans debating the GOAT (Greatest of All Time). No matter the reason, a rivalry game gives everyone something to root for.

Fans are passionate when it comes to supporting their favorite teams.

Liverpool FC and Manchester United face off on the field during a Premier League match.

Chapter 1

College Rivals

Some rivalries go way, way back. And college sports are no exception. Players give it their all on the field.

California Polytechnic State University (Cal Poly) vs. University of California, Santa Barbara (UCSB)

The greatest rivalry in college soccer is between the Cal Poly Mustangs and the UCSB Gauchos. The Blue-Green rivalry brings out passionate fans. Crowds are some of the largest in National Collegiate Athletic Association (NCAA) men's soccer. From 2011 to 2019, Cal Poly sold out every seat in their stadium for the game against UCSB.

The UCSB team celebrates after defeating their UCLA rivals.

The teams face off twice a year in the Big West Conference. Both are **fierce** competitors. 11 of their past 18 games have ended in a **draw** or have been decided by one goal. Since 2008, 14 of 28 games have gone into extra time.

In October 2007, Cal Poly won 2–1 after losing 12 games in a row to UCSB. Since then, this rivalry has kicked into high gear. Cal Poly came out on top again in 2018 but haven't won a matchup against UCSB since. Cal Poly has also never won an NCAA championship. UCSB achieved the top spot once in 2006.

Stats (as of 2021) ⚽

Total matchups (regular season): 53		
Cal Poly: 19	UCSB: 28	draw: 6

NCAA Championship wins	
Cal Poly: 0	UCSB: 1

Fun Fact

Cal Poly and UCSB are located less than 100 miles (161 kilometers) apart on the California coast. Since 1994, they have had six tie games. In five of those games, neither team scored.

Marquette University vs. University of Wisconsin-Milwaukee

You know competition is fierce when a rivalry has its own trophy! Every year, Marquette battles it out with the University of Wisconsin-Milwaukee (UWM). These rivals are only 4 miles (6 km) apart. They play each year to see who will take home the Milwaukee Cup.

The Milwaukee Cup goes to the winner of the annual UWM-Marquette game.

The competition started in 1973. Things really heated up in 2006. The UWM Panthers' head coach changed sides. He headed to Marquette to coach the Golden Eagles. Each team felt they had something to prove. In 2022, the Golden Eagles won the cup for the first time since 2014.

The Panthers celebrate after securing the Milwaukee Cup.

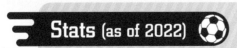

Stats (as of 2022) ⚽

Total matchups: 48		
Marquette: 12	UWM: 31	draw: 5

University of California, Los Angeles (UCLA) vs. University of Southern California (USC)

UCLA and USC have been rivals in every sport for the past 80 years. Their women's soccer teams are no different.

The teams have squared off on the field 28 times. UCLA has won 22 times. In 2007, the USC Trojans ended UCLA's eight-game winning streak. They defeated them in the semifinals. USC went on to win the NCAA Championship.

USC players gathered on the field to celebrate winning the 2007 Women's College Cup.

The tables turned in 2008. The teams battled it out in the NCAA quarterfinals. UCLA beat USC 1–0.

In November 2022, USC shut out UCLA 2–0 in the regular season finale. UCLA still went on to win the 2022 NCAA Tournament.

Stats (as of 2022) ⚽

NCAA Tournament appearances	
USC: 20	UCLA: 26
NCAA Championship wins	
USC: 2	UCLA: 2

Team USA players (from left to right) Natasha Kai, Lauren Cheney, and Amy Rodriguez pose with their gold medals.

Fun Fact

UCLA player Lauren Cheney teamed up with USC's Amy Rodriguez in the 2008 Summer Olympics in Beijing, China. Together, they helped win a gold medal for Team USA.

Chapter 2

World Cup Clashes

Every four years, teams from around the globe compete in the **FIFA World Cup**. Tensions can run high as national pride is at stake.

United States Women's National Team (USWNT) vs. Sweden

The USWNT is one of the best in the world. Sweden is their constant competitor. The relationship started off friendly. The two teams first played one another in the 1991 Women's World Cup. They stayed in the same hotel and even shared food early in the tournament.

The U.S. and Sweden faced off in the first Women's World Cup, held in 1991.

Fast forward to the 2016 Olympic quarterfinals. Sweden eliminated the U.S. in a prequalification game. Afterward, USWNT's Hope Solo called the Swedish team cowards for their strategy in the game. The friendly rivalry ended there.

Fierce competitors, the U.S. and Sweden have played against one another at five World Cups in a row. The U.S. won three games with one draw.

Players from USWNT and Sweden fight for control of the ball.

Alex Morgan vs. Christen Press

USWNT players Alex Morgan and Christen Press were once rivals themselves. Morgan led the UC Berkeley women's team to four NCAA Tournaments. Press played at Stanford and is a record holder with 71 goals. The two joined forces on the USWNT and helped win the 2019 World Cup.

United States vs. Mexico

Being neighbors doesn't stop these men's soccer teams from having an epic rivalry. At times, more than 100,000 fans have cheered on their matches. Their games have ended in team **brawls**. Coaches have been ejected. And in 2021, a U.S. team member was injured when a fan threw an object after the U.S. took the lead.

After the U.S.'s game-winning penalty kick in 2021, Mexico's fans were so upset they threw drinks at the winning team.

The U.S. team came out on top during the 2002 World Cup.

Mexico and the U.S. have met seven times at the Gold Cup finals since 1993. Mexico has won five of those games. The U.S. turned things around in 2002. They beat Mexico 2–0 during the World Cup round of 16 and moved on to the quarterfinals.

The win changed the rivalry. It showed Mexico that the U.S. was a team to take seriously. Since then, they've played 27 games. The U.S. has won 12. Mexico has won eight. Neither team has won a World Cup.

Stats (as of 2021) ⚽

Total matchups: 74		
Wins:		
Mexico: 36	U.S.: 22	draw: 16

Argentina vs. Brazil

The rivalry between Brazil and Argentina is the biggest in South American men's soccer. These two countries have never been fond of one another. Their games are filled with drama and passion.

Players from opposing teams argued during their 2018 World Cup matchup.

Brazil is the only country to have participated in every World Cup tournament to date. They've also won more World Cups than any other team. They've faced Argentina four times in the World Cup. Brazil won two of those matches.

Their games aren't without **controversy**. In 1990, Argentina beat Brazil 1–0. There were accusations that the Argentinians put a **tranquilizer** in the water bottle of one of the Brazilian players. In 2005, the Argentinian coach was interviewed about the incident. He said, "I'm not saying it didn't happen."

Stats (as of 2022) ⚽

Total matchups: 113

Argentina: 41	Brazil: 46	draw: 26

Goals scored

Argentina: 162	Brazil: 166

World Cup appearances

Argentina: 18	Brazil: 22

World Cup wins

Argentina: 3	Brazil: 5

World Cup matchups: 4

Argentina: 1	Brazil: 2	draw: 1

Chapter 3

Crosstown Competition

Whether teams are a few miles away or hours apart, hometown heroes can drive rivalries. Fans and players are passionate, and anything can happen on the field.

FC Barcelona vs. Real Madrid

The two biggest cities in Spain also have two of the biggest soccer teams. Real Madrid and Barcelona are two of the most successful clubs in the world. They're also two of the biggest rivals.

A fight broke out between players when Barcelona and Real Madrid faced off in 2010.

This rivalry dates back 120 years. Different politics and cultures play a big part. Their matchup even has its own name—El Clásico.

The two teams have been battling to be the best since they first faced off in 1902. Barcelona won 3–1. The biggest win in the series goes to Real Madrid, though. In 1943, they beat Barcelona 11–1.

Both teams have huge followings and **loyal** fans. After Luis Figo left Barcelona to join Real Madrid, fans were furious. One even threw a pig's head at Figo during a game in 2002.

Stats (as of 2022)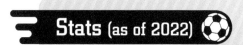

Total matchups: 249

Barcelona: 97   Real Madrid: 100   draw: 52

Famous players—Real Madrid

Cristiano Ronaldo, Iker Casillas, Alfredo Di Stéfano

Famous players—FC Barcelona

Lionel Messi, Ronaldinho (Ronaldo de Assis Moreira), Diego Maradona

Liverpool vs. Manchester United

Liverpool and Manchester are two of the most successful teams in England. Only 35 miles (56 km) apart, the two have been rivals for more than 120 years. The two first met on the field in 1894. Liverpool won the match 2–0.

Rivals get fierce and physical on the field.

Manchester United fans wave flags and banners to support their team.

Fans are passionate and so are players. Many have spoken about their dislike for the other team. In 1996, Liverpool's Neil Ruddock broke both legs of Manchester United's Andy Cole. Ruddock apologized, saying he only meant to break one.

Both teams are skilled competitors. Liverpool has won 67 major club titles. Manchester has 66.

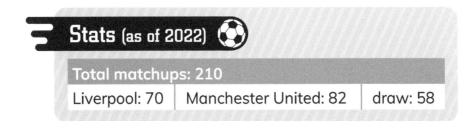

Stats (as of 2022) ⚽

Total matchups: 210

Liverpool: 70	Manchester United: 82	draw: 58

Los Angeles Galaxy vs. San Jose Earthquakes

Rivalries run just as deep in U.S. soccer. The competition between the LA Galaxy and San Jose Earthquakes also has its own name—the California Clásico.

This rivalry comes down to regional pride. The Galaxy have the glitz and glamour of Los Angeles. David Beckham played on the team! The Quakes represent the Bay Area. Winner takes the Western Conference and goes on to compete in the Major League Soccer (MLS) Cup.

David Beckham (left) is held back by a teammate during his time with the LA Galaxy.

Their 2003 matchup in the Conference Semifinals marks one of the best comebacks in MLS history. The Quakes trailed 4–0 in the second game of a two-game series. But they fought back, scoring three goals.

Just before time ran out, the Quakes scored again. The game went into extra time. The Quakes won 5–2. They went on to win the Cup that year.

An LA Galaxy forward pushes through the Earthquakes defense.

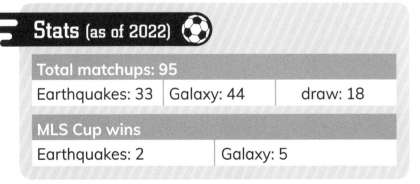

Stats (as of 2022) ⚽

Total matchups: 95		
Earthquakes: 33	Galaxy: 44	draw: 18
MLS Cup wins		
Earthquakes: 2	Galaxy: 5	

Chapter 4

Playing for MVP

Most players play to win. And almost all want the bragging rights that go along with being the best. That combination can lead to some intense rivalries.

Diego Maradona vs. Pelé

When it comes to soccer greats, Maradona and Pelé are often debated as the GOAT. Both started playing professionally at 15 and went on to become heroes in their countries: Maradona in Argentina and Pelé in Brazil.

Maradona (left) and Pelé are two of the best players of all time.

They both made history at the World Cup. At 17, Pelé became the youngest player to score in a World Cup Final and to win a World Cup. In 1986, Maradona became the only player to score and assist five goals in a single World Cup.

In 2000, they shared the honor of accepting FIFA's "Player of the Century" award. Maradona was not happy about it. He accepted his own award but left before Pelé received his.

Although the two never played against one another, that doesn't stop fans from comparing them. Some believe Maradona is the best overall player. Others say Pelé was the best league scorer. Either way, their stats prove both were incredible talents.

Career stats ⚽

	Maradona	Pelé
World Cup appearances	4	4
World Cup wins	1	3
Goals scored	338 in 619 games	775 (although some say more than 1,000) in 840 games
Career length	21 years	22 years

Cristiano Ronaldo vs. Lionel Messi

Fans have a hard time deciding who does it better—Al-Nassr FC's Cristiano Ronaldo or Paris Saint-Germain's Lionel Messi. Their former teams—FC Barcelona and Real Madrid—are rivals, so it's only natural for fans to compare the players.

Messi and Ronaldo are close in age and evenly matched. They're known as the best forwards in the league. So far, the two have played each other 36 times in their careers. Messi won 16 games. Ronaldo won 11 times. Nine games ended in a draw.

Ronaldo (left) and Messi try to beat each other to the ball.

Messi (left) takes Ronaldo's hand on the field.

Although these soccer stars are not friends, this is not a mean rivalry. The two are polite to one another.

Messi won a gold medal in the 2008 Olympics. In 2022, he won his first FIFA World Cup as part of Argentina's national team.

Stats (as of 2022) ⚽

	Messi	Ronaldo
Goals	781	817
Assists	339	231
Games played	989	1,134
World Cup wins	1	0
Career length	19 years	21 years

David Beckham vs. Diego Simeone

It was hate at first kick for David Beckham and Diego Simeone. Tensions were high between their teams—England and Argentina—during the second round of the 1998 World Cup Finals. The teams were tied 2–2. Then Simeone **fouled** Beckham, sending him to the ground.

Beckham kicked back, and Simeone played up his injury. The referee gave Beckham a **red card**. England was eliminated and lost their chance at victory.

A referee gives Beckham (center) a red card during the 1998 World Cup Finals.

Beckham's penalty kick helped win the game in 2002.

Four years later, the two teams met again at the 2002 World Cup. Beckham played it cool. He scored a penalty kick that helped England beat Argentina 1–0.

Career stats ⚽

	Beckham	Simeone
World Cup appearances	3	3
World Cup wins	0	0
World Cup goals scored	3	11

Glossary

brawl (BRAWL)—a rough fight

controversy (KON-truh-vur-see)—a public disagreement or dispute between groups of people

draw (DRAW)—a tie game or contest

fierce (FEERSS)—daring and dangerous

FIFA (FI-fuh)—the international governing body of soccer; FIFA stands for Fédération Internationale de Football Association

foul (FOUL)—an action that is against the rules

loyal (LOI-uhl)—being true to something or someone

red card (RED KAHRD)—results in an automatic ejection, the referee takes the player out of the remainder of the game for a violation

tranquilizer (TRANG-kwul-lye-zur)—a drug that has a calming effect

World Cup (WURLD CUP)—a soccer competition held every four years in a different country; teams from around the world compete against each other; Brazil has won the World Cup more times than any other country

Read More

Berglund, Bruce. *Big-Time Soccer Records.* North Mankato, MN: Capstone, 2022.

Jökulsson, Illugi. *Messi and Ronaldo: Who Is the Greatest?* New York: Abbeville Kids, 2020.

Keith, Tanya. *Soccer Stars on the Pitch: Biographies of Today's Best Players.* Emeryville, CA: Rockridge Press, 2019.

Internet Sites

Britannica Kids: World Cup
kids.britannica.com/kids/article/World-Cup/390872

Kiddle: FIFA World Cup facts for kids
kids.kiddle.co/FIFA_World_Cup

Sports Illustrated Kids: Soccer
sikids.com/tag/soccer

Index

About the Author

Dani Borden is a writer based in Los Angeles, California. She enjoys learning and researching new topics to write about. Previously a dog-person, she now has two cats and has been known to root for the Atlanta Braves.

photo credit: Leah Ford